Lerner SPORTS™

SPORTS VIPs

I0878793

MEET ANTHONY EDWARDS

MATT DOEDEN

Lerner Publications ◆ Minneapolis

SPORTS THRILLS MEET RESEARCH SKILLS

Lerner SPORTS

Free Database Trial: lernersports.com

Copyright © 2025 by Lerner Publishing Group, Inc.

All rights reserved. International copyright secured. No part of this book may be reproduced, stored in a retrieval system, or transmitted in any form or by any means—electronic, mechanical, photocopying, recording, or otherwise—without the prior written permission of Lerner Publishing Group, Inc., except for the inclusion of brief quotations in an acknowledged review.

Lerner Publications Company
An imprint of Lerner Publishing Group, Inc.
241 First Avenue North
Minneapolis, MN 55401 USA

For reading levels and more information, look up this title at www.lernerbooks.com.

Main body text set in Aptifer Slab LT Pro. Typeface provided by Linotype AG.

Editor: Nicole Berglund **Photo Editor:** Nicole Berglund
Lerner team: Sue Marquis

Library of Congress Cataloging-in-Publication Data

Names: Doeden, Matt, author.
Title: Meet Anthony Edwards : Minnesota Timberwolves superstar / Matt Doeden.
Description: Minneapolis, MN : Lerner Publications, [2026] | Series: Lerner sports. Sports VIPs | Includes bibliographical references and index. | Audience: Ages 7–11 years | Audience: Grades 4–6 | Summary: "Anthony Edwards is a two-time NBA All-Star. In 2020, he was selected by the Minnesota Timberwolves with the number one pick in the NBA draft. Readers learn more about the shooting guard's life and career"— Provided by publisher.
Identifiers: LCCN 2024028562 (print) | LCCN 2024028563 (ebook) | ISBN 9798765670859 (lib. bdg.) | ISBN 9798765670866 (paperback) | ISBN 9798765670880 (epub)
Subjects: LCSH: Edwards, Anthony, 2001-—Juvenile literature. | Guards (Basketball)—United States—Biography—Juvenile literature. | Basketball players—Georgia—Atlanta—Biography—Juvenile literature. | Minnesota Timberwolves (Basketball team)—Juvenile literature. | Basketball—Minnesota—Minneapolis—History—Juvenile literature.
Classification: LCC GV884.E427 D64 2026 (print) | LCC GV884.E427 (ebook) | DDC 796.323092 [B]—dc23/eng/20240812

LC record available at https://lccn.loc.gov/2024028562
LC ebook record available at https://lccn.loc.gov/2024028563

Manufactured in the United States of America
1-1011346-54104-9/6/2024

TABLE OF CONTENTS

TWO-WAY STAR

Denver Nuggets fans roared as their team brought the ball up the court. It was Game 1 of the 2024 Western Conference Semifinals. The Nuggets had won the NBA title the year before. They were favored to win the series. But the Minnesota Timberwolves were playing tough. Denver led 54–50 early in the third quarter.

Denver forward Michael Porter Jr. passed the ball to center Nikola Jokić. Porter quickly drove toward the rim as Jokić passed it back. It looked as if it would be an easy basket. But Wolves guard Anthony Edwards leaped in front of Porter for a huge block. The ball went right

FAST FACTS

DATE OF BIRTH: August 5, 2001
POSITION: shooting guard
LEAGUE: National Basketball Association (NBA)

PROFESSIONAL HIGHLIGHTS: was an NBA All-Star in 2023 and 2024; named to the All-NBA second team in 2024; scored a career-high 51 points on April 9, 2024, in a win over the Washington Wizards

PERSONAL HIGHLIGHTS: was a star running back in football as a child; made his acting debut in a 2022 film; his brother Antony is a rapper who goes by the name bdifferent

to Minnesota's Jaden McDaniels, who threw a long pass to forward Karl-Anthony Towns. Towns threw down a thunderous slam dunk to pull the Wolves to within two points.

The game remained close. The Wolves held an 82–81 lead with about seven minutes to go. Edwards dribbled the ball from beyond the three-point line. The Nuggets' Aaron Gordon was all over him. Edwards darted to his right. But Gordon was ready. He got in front of Edwards.

Edwards (*right*) drives toward the basket during the 2024 playoffs.

Edwards shoots the ball between two Denver defenders.

Edwards paused just inside the three-point line. Then he faked a drive to his left. Gordon took the bait. As the defender lunged in that direction, Edwards shifted right, jumped, and launched a shot. The ball touched nothing but net as it went through the rim!

Edwards was on fire. The 21-year-old scored 43 points and played amazing defense as the Wolves shocked the Denver crowd with a 106–99 victory. "There's no weaknesses in his game," Denver coach Michael Malone said of Edwards. "And it's going to be a . . . challenge trying to slow him down."

CHAPTER 1

GOALS AND TRAGEDIES

Anthony Edwards was born August 5, 2001, in Atlanta, Georgia (*pictured*). His father, Roger Caruth, didn't stay with the family. Anthony lived with his mother, Yvette Edwards, and three siblings, Antoinette, Antoine, and Antony. His grandmother, Shirley, was also a big part of the family. Caruth had another son, Rajah Caruth, who is Anthony's half brother.

From an early age, Anthony was a gifted athlete. He starred in baseball, football, and basketball. He dreamed of a future as a pro athlete. One day Anthony wrote a list of his goals, including becoming an NBA player. The problem was that he wrote them on a wall in his grandmother's house—in permanent marker!

Anthony plays at the Pangos All-American Camp, a basketball event for talented teenage players, in 2018.

Early on, it looked like football would be Anthony's sport. "I could have been a professional football player," he said. "I was really good. I was the [number one] running back in the country at the age of 9 or 10. I stopped playing because I [saw] my brothers playing basketball. I thought it looked more fun."

Anthony played against his brothers day after day. The older boys always beat him. He was strong and quick, but he wasn't a great shooter. So he kept working. He vowed to win someday.

Anthony (*left*) plays for his high school in 2019.

SUPER SPORTS SCOOP

Anthony's father wasn't a big part of his life. But Caruth gave his son the nickname Ant-Man. It's a nickname that has followed Anthony through childhood and into the NBA.

Tragedy struck when Anthony was 14. His mother died from cancer. Months later, cancer also took his grandmother. It was a pair of crushing blows for him. He still speaks little of his struggles at that time. It's a very private matter to him.

Anthony's siblings stepped in to raise him. Sports were at the center of their lives. The brothers kept playing basketball in their spare time, and Anthony finally started winning when he was in ninth grade.

CHAPTER 2

TOP DOG

As a teenager, Anthony was a powerhouse on the court at Holy Spirit Preparatory School. He loved to slash to the rim. He could throw down massive slam dunks. In 2018, as a junior, he led his school to a state championship. As a senior, he averaged 29 points per game.

College scouts noticed. Several scouting services ranked him as the top player in the nation. He had his pick of colleges, including Kansas, North Carolina, and Kentucky. But Edwards decided to stay close to home. He chose the University of Georgia so he could work with coach Tom Crean.

Edwards plays for the University of Georgia in 2020.

Edwards graduated from high school in 2019. That fall, he headed to Athens, Georgia, to join the University of Georgia Bulldogs. Soon he proved that he belonged. Edwards scored 24 points in his first game! Edwards thrived even against the best teams. When Georgia faced Michigan State, Edwards scored 37 points in a close loss. Michigan State was ranked as the third-best college team in the US at the time.

It was a season of mixed results for Edwards. His numbers were great. He averaged 19.1 points per game.

SUPER SPORTS SCOOP

Both Edwards's mother and grandmother died on the fifth day of the month. Edwards wears number 5 on his jersey to honor their memories.

Edwards throws down a dunk in 2020 while playing for Georgia.

But the Bulldogs struggled as a team. They finished with a 5–13 record in their conference.

Days after the season ended, Edwards announced that he would leave Georgia to enter the NBA draft. NBA scouts and coaches weren't sure what to think of him. Some saw him as the best player in the draft. He had the strength and speed to be an NBA star. But others weren't so sure. His college team had not been good.

CHAPTER 3

WELCOME TO THE NBA

The Timberwolves had the number one pick in the 2020 NBA draft. It was an unusual year. COVID-19 had forced the NBA to delay the draft five months. When the Wolves finally got to make their choice, no one was sure who it would be.

They chose Edwards. He had some things to work on. But his raw talent was just too good to pass up. Edwards watched the draft at home, with pictures of his mother and grandmother beside him. "It was a blessing, it was a dream come true," Edwards said. "I'm just happy to be here and I'm blessed to be in this position."

Edwards practices before a game in 2021.

COVID-19 delayed the 2020–2021 NBA season. Usually, rookies get a training camp to adjust to the league. But Edwards and the other rookies that year didn't have that benefit. The NBA skipped training camp to get straight to the season. The rookies had to learn on the fly.

In his first game, Edwards scored 15 points in a Wolves win. But it wasn't an easy start. He struggled to find good

SUPER SPORTS SCOOP

Edwards acted in a film in 2022. The movie stars Adam Sandler, who plays a basketball scout, and Juancho Hernangómez as a young player. Edwards plays Kermit Wilts, the rival of Hernangómez's character. Many people who saw the film praised Edwards's performance.

Edwards drives with the ball during a 2021 game against the Utah Jazz.

shots. He had trouble knowing where he was supposed to be on defense.

Edwards got better and better as the season went on. On May 5, 2021, he scored a season-high 42 points in a close loss to the Memphis Grizzlies. He finished the season averaging 19.3 points per game and was second to LaMelo Ball in the NBA's Rookie of the Year voting.

Edwards kept working. In 2021–2022, he improved his shooting and scored 21.3 points per game. He was an even better defender. He helped the Wolves reach the playoffs and scored 36 points in his first playoff game, leading to a win over the Grizzlies. The Wolves lost the series. But Edwards's rise was giving Wolves fans a reason to believe that the team was getting better.

Edwards attends an event for his movie in Los Angeles, California, in 2022.

Edwards shoots the ball during the 2022 playoffs.

CHAPTER 4

SUPERSTAR

Edwards's play improved in the 2022–2023 season. He averaged 24.6 points per game and made his first NBA All-Star team. He led the Wolves to the play-in tournament. If they could beat the New Orleans Pelicans, the Wolves would be in the playoffs. Edwards scored 26 points and had four steals and four blocks in a win over the Pelicans. He helped the Wolves reach the playoffs.

In the playoffs, they faced the powerful Denver Nuggets. Edwards played great in the series. He averaged 31.6 points per game. But Denver was too strong. They won the series 4–1 and went on to claim the NBA championship.

Edwards dunks the ball in the 2023 NBA All-Star Game.

SUPER SPORTS SCOOP

Edwards was a top scorer for Team USA at the 2023 FIBA Basketball World Cup. In 2024, he played for the US men's basketball team at the Olympic Games in Paris, France. They took home the gold medal!

By 2023–2024, Edwards was a rising superstar. The Wolves were one of the best teams that season. Edwards took a big step forward, averaging 25.9 points per game. The Wolves faced the Phoenix Suns in the first round of the playoffs. Phoenix had a loaded team, including one of Edwards's heroes, Kevin Durant. Edwards torched Durant and the Suns. The Wolves swept the series to advance.

Next, they had a rematch with the powerful Nuggets. Edwards and the Wolves dominated the first two games.

But Denver stormed back to win the next three. In Game 6, Edwards's brother Antony, a rapper who goes by bdifferent, performed during the halftime show. The Wolves came out strong to win the game. Then, in Game 7, the Wolves used amazing defense to win.

Edwards drives past a Denver Nuggets player during the 2024 playoffs.

Edwards looks for an open teammate to pass the ball to during the 2024 playoffs.

The magical season ended there. Edwards and the Wolves lost the Western Conference Finals to the Dallas Mavericks. But the team made great progress. Edwards, at just 22, had already stepped up as one of the NBA's biggest stars. Basketball fans can't wait to see what's next for the young superstar.

Edwards goes up for a slam dunk in a 2024 game.

ANTHONY EDWARDS CAREER STATS

GAMES:

302

POINTS:

6,920

ASSISTS:

1,241

REBOUNDS:

1,567

STEALS:

413

THREE-POINTERS:

789

Stats are accurate through the 2023–2024 NBA season.

GLOSSARY

COVID-19: a disease that emerged in late 2019 and spread around the world

draft: when teams take turns choosing new players

drive: to move forcefully toward the basket

guard: a player stationed in the backcourt

play-in tournament: games played at the end of each NBA season to decide the final two playoff teams

rim: the edge of a basketball hoop

rookie: a first-year player

scout: a person who judges the skills of athletes

slam dunk: a shot in basketball made by jumping high into the air and throwing the ball down through the basket

slash: a quick, driving motion toward the basket

SOURCE NOTES

7 AP, "Edwards Scores 43 Points, Reid Erupts in 4th to Help Timberwolves Beat Nuggets 106–99 in Game 1," ESPN.com, May 4, 2024, https://www.espn.com/nba/recap/_/gameId/401657182.

10 Ricky O'Donnell, "The Origin Story of High School Basketball's 'Ant-Man,'" SBNation, January 15, 2019, https://www.sbnation.com/college-basketball/2019/1/15/18139281/anthony-edwards-basketball-recruiting-nba-draft.

17 "NBA Draft Show: Anthony Edwards Interview," Facebook video, November 19, 2020, https://www.facebook.com/watch/?v=290001448991388.

LEARN MORE

Flynn, Brendan. *The NBA Encyclopedia for Kids*. Minneapolis: Abdo Reference, 2022.

Jr. NBA
https://jr.nba.com

Leed, Percy. *Pro Basketball by the Numbers*. Minneapolis: Lerner Publications, 2025.

Minnesota Timberwolves
https://www.nba.com/timberwolves

Sports Illustrated Kids: Basketball
https://www.sikids.com/basketball

Whiting, Jim. *The Story of the Minnesota Timberwolves*. Mankato, MN: Creative Education, 2023.

INDEX

PHOTO ACKNOWLEDGMENTS

Image credits: AP Photo/Melissa Tamez/Icon Sportswire, p. 4; Matthew Stockman/Getty Images, p. 6; AP Photo/David Zalubowski, p. 7; imageBROKER.com GmbH & Co. KG/Alamy, p. 8; AP Photo/Brian Rothmuller/Icon Sportswire, p. 9; Kevin Liles/Getty Images, pp. 10, 12; AP Photo/Kristin M. Bradshaw/Athens Banner-Herald, p. 13; Tribune Content Agency LLC/Alamy, p. 15; Steph Chambers/Getty Images, p. 16; Mitchell Leff/Getty Images, p. 17; AP Photo/Adam Fondren, p. 19; Variety/Getty Images, p. 20; AP Photo/Brandon Dill, p. 21; Christian Petersen/Getty Images, pp. 22, 26; Pool/Getty Images, p. 23; C. Morgan Engel/Stringer/Getty Images, p. 25; AP Photo/Matt Krohn, p. 27. Design elements: Tamjaii9/Shutterstock; The Hornbills Studio/Shutterstock.

Cover: AP Photo/Abbie Parr.